THE KADUPUL FLOWER

THE KADUPUL FLOWER

— A POEM BY EC —

EC

ISBN-13: 9780692760543
ISBN-10: 0692760547

INTRODUCTION

L ife is like poetry, poetry in motion, inspired by love
and the love of devotion.

DEDICATION

To my father, mother, friends and love ones

AMBER AND SILK

Forgetting her true self, nourishing her heart's desire, we both stripped off our clothes, to bathe near noon. For her skin, lilies the beauty of spring, laughter of youth, smile of truth. I gazed, my spirit wondering in the field above the countryside, and you the song on thy lips, the sweetness of wine, the most beautiful of silk, the altar which many a man prays, the goddess. My heart desires your body in its human form. Within her flesh, her bones of Ivory are caressed with the poisons of life's darkest whispers. The tears of the fire queen burns as the golden amber sun in the season of her reign. Naked souls bare nothing uncovering truths, and here in her naked form, nothing seems as once was, the bitter now sweet, the strong once weak, I alone hear the voices of angels when they speak.

FRAILTY

Her beauty, such the beauty of elegance.
The sight of her sets hearts ablaze. Passion, a furnace
within my heart. Ravish her, my love so eloquent. At first
I tried to control these thoughts, but then I recalled her
face, those hands, her gestures. Frailty, if only she could
read these thoughts. Heaven, paradise on earth, within
her I get lost.

VALENTINE

Venice Italy. I, alone with her natural beauty. I pray, may sleep be the only thing to part our love. With my confidence, and your smarts, we shall conquer Rome. You are as sweet as the syrup we pour over the pancakes of hearts, as brave as a Warrior Queen, as holy as the Virgin, pure as snow. On this Valentine's Day, may cupid guide us with God's grace forevermore.

AS TIMES CHANGE

As the times change, our love shall evolve,
We danced all night, living within that moment.
At the drive-in, we watch romance. How beautiful the spotlight on you loving me.
As the times changed, we grew knowing a little bit more, emotions have matured.
Ask of me, how much do I?
I replied, it would be my honor to fall upon the sword of mercy and suffer a lifetime of anguish pain and misery. She stands the test of times, her heartbeat believing in the innocence of poetry until the end of times. As times will change.

THE WEDDING VOW

The universe has answered my prayers, here I stand with you on this day.

A star guiding hearts from creation we've become, space and time only remains my virtuous bride.

You have given life to me as you had in lives before. Honor, trust, I will not forsake. And when the hands of age caress your beauty taking what it had loan, and strength flees leaving me frail as old bones,

I shall stand with you on that day as now I do, pleading with the masters of the hereafter to take me first, as how now I am taking you.

EAT AND DRINK

Searching for my lover through the city streets I roamed, she takes me by force.

And I ate, becoming drunk with love.

I am invited to sit in her garden, the sensual taste of her fruits. I knock, she was slow to open. I spoke with tenderness until she became my truth. I am darkened because of the sun in my city, guided by the touch of God and you, thy fountain which quenches the cities of God.

LAVENDER

The road to my heart lies open, yet in her sadness she could not be any more beautiful. She told me a tale that took my breath away, and it was all true. At last we are made whole by the intricacies of time, but only to lose ourselves once more to her power divine. Her eyes are beauty which beholds beautiful things, her soul the scent of lavender fragrances throughout the kingdoms of kings.

HER LAND OF MILK AND HONEY

In the depths of sorrow, solace, the graveyard of forgotten hearts, lovers' bitter quarrels, the truth only burns when spoken from my lover's heart. I would rather live within my own hell being free, than in heaven being a slave to thee. With her warm embrace the emotions of life vividly awakens, awaiting the deity of dark romance. His violence and sex which drips of honey, the milk of life my chamber awaits my lover to be beautifully sacrificed.

THIS TRAGIC WAR

It is love that brings me to your city gates, you are brave my love. Sleeping with my enemy while defending my faith, her fears are the flames which I dare to walk through, fire and the sword. We bathe in blood, a price to make the many whole. Power to win her heart's desire, but can desire be all? Her intricate complexities, beauty everlasting, trapped inside of her labyrinth forever, fighting her tragic war.

22

Life is more than just self, as the bigger picture reveals. More than markets, something that numbers cannot conceive. Life isn't selfish, she does not deceive.

She's the beauty that's abundant if you choose to see, the breeze which blows you for me. Life is everywhere from the skies to the sea.

PHONETIC

The only heaven I am trying to find is her face, and if heaven is as beautiful as this, may I dwell in the Ruca Malen eating of her fruits, drinking of her flesh, awakening to her naked desires, exploring my thoughts as I explore her hidden sanctuaries. With you my love, my love grows stronger. The bittersweet moments that shall forever be no more, cradled within our eternal happiness, forever and forever more.

LAWLESS LOVE

In all her tears, are the flowers of youth.
Her joy became his sins, the pleasures of my sins. Flames
which are forbidden, my heart became the fire to her vio-
lence, within our anguish letters of passion perverted my
thoughts. Here I am, boy love struck by youth, girl with
thoughts of shame, the Gods who am I to blame. I have
over indulged in the lust of piety, sin in the ways of truth.
Now I find myself in your soft embrace, revealing what
has been locked behind lips. Concealed beauty needs no
proof, powers of thy word lovers of the truth

THE ART OF WAR (JAPANESE)

Kanojo putto Inkurudo Atsuryoku Ni,
Ika no yona shiatsu ji bun no
Nihongo Koibito watash shimesa remashita
Kanojo no Atarshi Tekunikku Bendo kanojo no Kozan
Sei kanojo no Karado Yowai, Wareware Shiyo-Zumi no
Yaku a Shukan ni inkurudo Shima Shikoku a Chisai
sukoshi Basho Sei Watashitachi no Hoho Mawarini
Matsuyama, Daberukoto sushi Ni a Osoroshidesu pesu,
Ni yoru wareware
Deshou shisen Appu Ni Inkurudo Hoshi,
Kiite iru Ni Kanojo no Tetsugaku Kanojo no
Shinri Kanojo no Gen'in, Kanojo Katamui Oba Soshite
Sasayaki, Chinmoku kimi no Kyofu
Tame Ni Nomi Ohiru Shitteimasu hoho Sukoshi ware-
ware Arimasu,

SELF EROTICA

The pleasure is all mine
For who knows me better than I
I connect with my flower deep and divine
The spring in my forest flows of a fountain. I tasted the
sweet aroma of blue strawberries
Wets my thighs. Of you I think, bringing the wildest of
erotica out in me. Spirit body and mind, the feelings are
overwhelming. Nirvana has taken control, for a moment,
a sweet moment is all it took
Words may not fully convey, as I lie here euphoric in
myself erotica

THE ROOT OF LOVE

You must love the song lyric, words of the poem. Without a voice, how must we find home.

I have traveled long and far, now I thirst for a sip of your deliverance.

My soul overflowed as joy filled the void of our tabernacle, lady in the shadows. Upon her night seas we have sailed, for conquest and gold.

Now rumors of wars upon our shores, and fight we must. For men only remember those of valor. For her I lay my heart down, victory in the face of fire.

My love, brave blood for country in honor I die, if you shall not live. The poison on a lover's lips. The depth which I sink without her, bottomless is my ocean.

Chain to bones in the dungeon of my enemy's soul, the smell of rotting flesh, the agony of heartless brutality, thy love has kept me warm.

The executioner's breath, I feel no more.

She lays motionless, her tears know the bitter truth, one cannot live without one's root.

ANGEL HEART

My angel and her heart
Her wings they sing a prayer to the father of glory
My angel and her heart
A song which makes beauty weep
My angel and her heart
The choirs magnificently adorn
My angel and her heart
The hallways of gracefulness
Marble sculptures, a sight to behold
My angel and her heart
We are sheltered where love dwells
And melodies of string instruments
Play the songs of inspirations that shower
Me
My angel and her heart

ROMANTICIZE NOSTALGIA

I would like to believe, we are set on a course of doomed faith, dying love and perpetual pain, swearing it's all from above. A mixture of emotions that cannot and will never make sense before she's too late. Who will survive her strangeness, a star in my outer Galaxy of darkness. She emerges, the sensations are momentarily the blissful truth. God only cares for the beautiful in her youth. Everything matters, so I romanticize lying beneath her covers. Nostalgia, a feeling of the dead past, embracing her for the moment, knowing as well this too shall past.

THE MOSAIC

My lover is tender, intimate in her mood. My story of idealized lust, the games we play, romantic but shrewd, a love affair speaking in the language of broken hearts, As we began, my lips felt the shivers of her heart. My soul begs the question, what form of nervousness is this? Susceptible to romance, afraid of losing my grip. A mosaic, to see her beauty makes me whole, antiquity's grace, the kiss reveals the passions which burn within our souls.

THE BOY KING

Power, lust, wanting, desire and sin.

Thoughts rage within the young boy king. He finds himself alone and afraid, but yet shows no signs.

Her desire for power leads her to sin, wanting nothing more. She admires the young boy king, she is as gold something new to his senses, lust enters.

As he slept, with thoughts of her great pleasures, the poison encourages him to follow the lady in the shadows. She watches as he struggles, a power which overcame kings. A Queen is crowned, giving birth, to a young boy king.

I JUST WANT TO BE UNDERSTOOD

I understand that. Who wants to be hurt? As long as I can remember, every guy I've met, from the first grade on up until now, just wanted one thing, for you to be their first.

With their smoother then smooth lines,

Fast sports cars, oh and my personal favorite, I'm a trust fund baby! You can trust me baby, I've seen them all. I don't want you to believe that I am ungrateful. I love my life!

It's giving me much to do, see and believe in, but this department of romance. Hmm, I'm not quite so sure. I've all but given up on this notion of happily ever after

What I am trying to say is, love is cool, sex is great! But at times, I just want to be understood.

SLEEPING BEAUTY

Hopes, wishes and dreams
Life and love divided, wants and needs separated
I gave heart, she gives warmth
Tenderness at the mercies of charm
A little bit of aspiration, imagination, I stirred the bubbling pot. As I turned the page, the recipe called for a princess' kiss. I pondered for a moment, where could I find this? At the utmost heights of worlds unknown I see irresistible those lips, the elixir a potion I poured between her dying lips
She gagged, reflexes animated her dead limbs. My lover lives once more throughout history, a fairytale retold as a myth, awakening my sleeping beauty

THE COURAGE OF LOVE

Deep within the heart of Brooklyn, they say true love shall never die. I'm ashamed of the way things went south, can you find the courage to give me another try? It has been said, that all the money in the world cannot buy true love. I guess these are the facts of life, so here is my heart as a down payment for my one true love in this life.

THE WHITE WITCH

In her stillness of midnight, I search for her dark mysteries
Her silk robe unfastened
Her hair upon her shoulders has fallen loose
The art of her magic spellbinding, she whispers in my
ear her darkest truths
I devour what is mine, as well you shall be consumed

BEAUTIFUL BLACK WOMEN

Beautiful black women, nothing is more beautiful than your beautiful blackness
Beautiful black girls, no strength stronger than your will
Ladies of color, I respect your courage, your might, grace and power.

THE TRAVELERS

A traveler on her travels, in seek of Enlightenment,
approached by a traveler on his journey, seeking truth
Where philosophies and ideas meet, reason gives way to
skepticism, rage and anger, doubt and fear
Hope intersects, bringing faith with joy, as meaningful
as love to a little baby boy.

BLOOD MOON

The bitterness of her bite never forgives, here in my moment of weakness she will forever live. Spurned by God's guilt, worthy of thy love to give. I hid my face in her presence. Passion you know it not, until my chambers you have shared. She caresses the broken, as they gaze upon this blood moon. I could feel the trembling in her heart where pain is momentary. Her love is the light which brings forth the blessings to sight.

THE TREE

My Cleopatra poison, eternal as the sphinx. Beauty which is everlasting, a power which overcame kings. Sensual incestuous unity of thy Queen, fear not the reasoning of our desires. For out of the stone, water and fire. She stood naked as the summer breeze, young spring in the mystic mood of prophecy, a love black as pitch. I asked myself, what form of wizardry is this? As I spoke, she adhered to my words, a spell I once conjured, wish I shall never tell. I ate from the tree of incest, her fruits were sweet. Indulged within her thoughts, I pray we find peace

AGE AIN'T NOTHING BUT A NUMBER

I made love to an older woman today, her beauty took my breath away. She was playful, tender, her touch made me feel as if we would be pleasured by this moment forever. I made love to a beautiful older woman today, astonishing blue eyes with a sparkle of gray. She taught me how to be patient with a lady. What's your rush she whispered? Pay attention and learn every inch of me, as we frolicked and made erotic sounds. I made love to a radiant older woman today. She was as sweet as fine aged wine. I learned how to take my time. Love making is beyond physical, the gateway to her mind, her gracefulness. In her arms, I felt as a boy coming into manhood. I made love to a beautiful beautiful older woman today.

THE ATMOSPHERE

The beauty of her soul, it's chilly kinda cold. Warm nights, her atmosphere screaming for attention, and you, the center. That star which everything revolves around, my landscape drapes orangutan bathing apes. Soul searching I guess, for something priceless, nothing less. I'm at the point of no return. This black hole only gets deeper, and my emotions run deep. So I take my time, taking my time with time. I'll leave you with this poem, and a few thoughts. I cannot give you the world, but I can show you life in all her simplicities.

HAI.KU

There is a hunger within me, my appetite for your desire knows no boundaries. Fearless, ferocious, chance without consequences, my kind of game. You are a timeless beauty, a sequence out of order but so correct. So let us not neglect what opportunity has thrust upon us, the HAI.KU.

Our days blew by fast, as if they were thoughts unchecked, a widow priest and kamikaze.

Letters written to a lover in the simplest of thoughts, words of her HAI.KU.

It is the century of the Great War, in the year nineteen four one. My love, you are the flower which grows beneath the waters of the great city of the hanging gardens, a wonder of all worlds. Her most intimate thoughts are camouflaged from all but he, behind the vail you see what others cannot see. I am sent on the first wave. My orders, make sure you aim for her heart.

DANCE THE NIGHT AWAY

Today I got paid, I could put a few bucks away. Me and my girlfriend on the beach, this feels like heaven to me. We can bathe in the sun, it's so beautiful to be young. Watching time slip on by, just living young and carefree. So tonight we will dance, take a risk take a chance. These are the moments of life, let's live them good, live them right. Baby it's just me and you, we'll take on this world. You'll be the Bonnie to my Clyde, and I'll be the lover of your world. So tonight we will dance, take a risk take a chance, leaving nothing up to faith, just place your hand within my hands.

NERDY SEXY GEEKS

I enjoy black hippie chicks, slim but tall, with well-defined hips.

I enjoy black hipster girls, with natural hair, puffy like an Afro with curls.

I enjoy nerdy sexy geeks, you know the ones who talk with their hands when they speak.

I enjoy beautiful toes. A lady who keeps it clean, her scent is of violets and rose.

I enjoy a lady who plays hard to get. Like a song that's memorable, she's hard to forget.

IF YOUR HEART BLEEDS.

If your heart bleeds, let it bleed for me never more, the muse without the artist. She walks away only to walk back, he leaves only for her to take him back. Something like a broken record, over the rainbow and shit. My pot of gold chained to her reckless soul. Damn, your love is cold, frost bites, the coldest lips on a frosty winter night. Think we took that condom off on spite. Despite the risk, she begs for this stiff dick, under my tonic rum and coke, listening to the best of the dramatics, the syndicates many lovers ago. I promised never to love the way I love this moment. I place my faith in love. Can she get over the fact that I'm a thug? I give her gangsta love from the back, she cries. Your pleasure is my sweetest pain, I go deep. Traveling through time like quantum leap physics, she wants to see if I'm a gimmick. I'm just an island boy, making love to her soul on my own island boy. Vintage, dare to dream. The Lord is my shepherd, judge me oh Lord, examine my heart. I touch her in ways, parting her thighs such as the Red Sea, dreaming of me and jubilee.

Made in the USA
Middletown, DE
19 June 2021